Roam Free: The Ultimate Guide to Staying Connected on Your RV Adventures

Wes "Wheels" Wheeler

Published by Fancy Free Living LLC, 2024.

ROAM FREE: THE ULTIMATE GUIDE TO STAYING CONNECTED ON YOUR RV ADVENTURES

First edition. April 8, 2024.

ISBN: 979-8224397860

Written by Wes "Wheels" Wheeler.

Table of Contents

Chapter 1

Important SIMPLE Definitions

If you are already familiar with the definitions used on the Internet and your phone, you probably don't need to read this chapter. But if you don't understand them, please read and understand these definitions before proceeding. I use them often in the eBook, as do all Internet providers. There are further definitions in Appendix A.

1.1 Internet Is a Group of Computers

The Internet is a vast collection of private, public, business, academic, and government systems built on computers that provide communication and data services. There is no single computer or location that makes up the Internet.

1.2 Wi-Fi is a Wireless Network

Wi-Fi is a wireless network that connects devices such as computers, TVs, and smartphones, usually to the Internet.

1.3 Router Connects Networks

A router is a device that connects two or more networks. It serves two primary functions: managing traffic (like a Crossing guard) and allowing multiple devices to connect. Most routers now enable communication wirelessly or through a hard wire called an Ethernet cable.

1.4 Modem Connects to the Telephone Line or Other Communication Channels

It converts signals from your computer or other devices into signals that can be transmitted over the telephone line or other communication channels. Nowadays, most Routers have a modem built in.

1.5 Satellite Internet Like Hughes and StarLink

Services like StarLink and Hughes have satellites in the sky that create a high-speed connection between devices like smartphones or computers and the Internet.

1.6 Hotspot Is a Wireless Connection

A Hotspot is a wireless device that lets you connect to another device. For example, your phone Hotspot allows you to connect to a computer or a TV, giving those items full access to the Internet.

1.7 Bluetooth Technology

Bluetooth technology allows devices to communicate with each other without cables or wires. For example, your phone may connect to a speaker or earphone to transmit a call. Bluetooth relies on short-range radio frequency; any device incorporating the technology can communicate as long as it is within the required distance.

1.8 Throttling Can Lower the Quality of Your Service

Internet Service Providers may intentionally slow down customers' service to limit the total amount of bandwidth consumed. This, in turn, can allow ISPs to minimize network congestion or charge more for the privileges of higher bandwidth. Internet throttling is most familiar with mobile and wireless ISPs. Look over the small print in any contract you sign, as it should be spelled out.

Chapter 2

Understanding RV Internet Needs

Before delving into the intricacies of RV internet technology, it's crucial to understand RVers' diverse and evolving needs for connectivity. From remote work and entertainment streaming to navigation and communication with loved ones, RVers rely on internet access for various purposes. This chapter explores the multiple scenarios where RVers require internet connectivity and delves into the factors influencing their connectivity needs.

2.1 Remote Work and Digital Nomadism

The rise of remote work (much due to the pandemic) and people wanting to move from place to place has transformed how people approach employment and travel. RVers who work remotely depend on reliable internet access to conduct virtual meetings, collaborate on projects, and access cloud-based tools and resources. Whether parked at a campground, boondocking in the wilderness, or traveling down the highway, RVers require stable internet connections to stay productive and connected with their professional networks.

2.2 Entertainment and Streaming

In addition to work-related tasks, RVers seek internet connectivity for entertainment purposes. Streaming movies, TV shows, and music via platforms like Netflix, Hulu, and Spotify have become a popular pastime for RVers during downtime. Reliable internet access allows them to enjoy their favorite content without interruptions, enhancing the overall RVing experience and providing entertainment options for individuals and families alike.

2.3 Navigation and Trip Planning

Modern RV navigation relies heavily on internet-connected devices and applications. GPS navigation systems, mapping apps, and trip-planning tools help RVers navigate unfamiliar routes, find campgrounds, locate points of interest, and avoid road hazards and traffic congestion. Internet access enables real-time updates and information, ensuring smooth and efficient travel experiences for RVers.

2.4 Communication and Social Connectivity

Staying connected with friends, family, and fellow RVers is essential for maintaining social ties and fostering community. RVers rely on internet-based communication tools such as email, social media, messaging apps, and video calls to stay in touch with loved ones, share travel experiences, and coordinate meetups and gatherings. Internet connectivity facilitates meaningful connections and interactions, even when RVers are thousands of miles away from RV.

2.5 Online Learning and Skill Development

Internet access opens online learning opportunities for RVers seeking personal and professional growth. Whether pursuing homeschooling options for their children, formal education for themselves, acquiring new skills, or engaging in lifelong learning, RVers can access many educational resources, courses, tutorials, and online webinars. Internet connectivity empowers RVers to continue their educational journeys on the road, regardless of location or schedule.

2.6 Safety and Emergency Communication

In emergencies, reliable internet access can be a lifeline for RVers. Whether seeking assistance, accessing emergency services, or communicating with authorities and first responders, internet connectivity enables quick and effective responses to unforeseen circumstances. RVers rely on internet-connected devices such as smartphones, GPS trackers, and emergency alert systems to stay informed and safe while traveling.

<u>Stay Flexible</u>: Embrace spontaneity and be open to adjusting your plans based on weather, road conditions, and unexpected "opportunities" that arise during your travels. Many RVers hate when things get changed. It leads to frustration and anxiety. Take a minute, laugh about it, see how important it is, and then examine if it is a problem or "an opportunity." We don't have much control over many things we as RVers encounter. Even the best-laid plans...

Q. What's an RVer's favorite dance move?

A. The Slide-Out!

Simple RV Honey & Mustard Recipe

Ingredients:

Two chicken breasts

1/4c Honey

1/4c Dijon Mustard

Capers (optional)

Steps:

You can marinate the chicken a few hours before
cooking, but it is unnecessary.

If using a marinade, put the chicken in a sealed bag with
the ingredients, and with your hands outside the bag,
work the marinade into the chicken.

When ready to cook, remove the chicken from the
marinade if you used one. Either way, whisk together the
honey and mustard in a small bowl. If you enjoy capers,
add them for a zestier taste.

Season the chicken with salt and pepper, and place in a
baking pan.

Pour the honey mustard sauce over the chicken and bake at 375 degrees for 25-30 minutes or until the chicken is cooked.

Serve with your favorite side dish or salad.

Simple marinade:

Mix oil, lemon juice, soy sauce, balsamic vinegar, brown sugar, Worchester sauce, garlic, salt, and pepper.

Chapter 3

The Evolution of RV Internet Technology

In the early days of Recreational Vehicle (RV) travel, connectivity was a luxury rather than a necessity. RVers relied on limited communication options such as AM/FM radio, CB radios, and occasional cellular signals where available. However, as technology advanced and society increasingly relied on the internet, the demand for reliable connectivity on the road surged. This chapter traces the fascinating evolution of RV internet technology, highlighting key milestones and innovations that have shaped the modern RVing experience.

3.1 Early Connectivity Challenges

In the early to mid-20th century, RVers faced significant challenges in staying connected while on the road. Communication options were limited, with AM/FM radios providing sporadic entertainment and CB radios facilitating essential short-range communication between vehicles. Cellular networks were virtually non-existent in rural and remote areas, leaving RVers isolated from the outside world for extended periods.

3.2 Emergence of Satellite Communication

The introduction of satellite communication revolutionized RV connectivity in the late 20th century. Satellite phones and data terminals enabled RVers to access voice and internet services in remote locations where traditional cellular networks were unavailable. While satellite communication offered unparalleled coverage, it came with high costs and technical complexities, limiting its widespread adoption among RV enthusiasts.

3.3 Rise of Cellular Connectivity

The advent of cellular technology marked a significant turning point in RV connectivity. As cellular networks expanded and became more robust, RVers gained access to reliable voice and data services across vast stretches of the country. The introduction of smartphones and mobile hotspots further democratized internet access, empowering RVers to stay connected on the go.

3.4 Evolution of Wi-Fi Technology

Wi-Fi technology revolutionized how RVers access the internet while parked at campgrounds, RV parks, and other public spaces. Wi-Fi access points were initially scarce, and connectivity could have been faster and more reliable. However, advancements in Wi-Fi technology, including the proliferation of high-speed networks and the development of long-range antennas and signal boosters, have vastly improved the RV Wi-Fi experience.

3.5 Smart Devices

Integrating Smart devices and innovative technology has enhanced the RVing experience. Smart RVs with connected appliances, thermostats, security systems, and entertainment devices offer RVers unprecedented convenience and control. Sensors and monitoring systems provide real-time data on RV systems and environmental conditions, enhancing safety and efficiency on the road.

3.6 The Role of Digital Nomadism

The rise of digital nomadism has fueled the demand for robust RV internet solutions. As more individuals embrace remote work and location-independent lifestyles, reliable connectivity becomes essential for maintaining productivity and staying connected with colleagues and clients on the road. RV internet technology is pivotal in enabling digital nomads to pursue professional endeavors while exploring the world in their mobile RVs.

Q. What is the best part about living in an RV?
A. It's harder for relatives to drop in for a visit

Chapter 4

What Is It That You Need?

4.1 What to Consider When Choosing

Now, we get into the nuts and bolts of finding the best Internet options for you. Don't let it be overwhelming. You will see on some future pages a simple way of deciding which is best for you. If you would like assistance finding and determining what is best for you, please email me at **info@FancyFreeLiving.com**, and I would be glad to help. I usually answer within 24 hours, and it may take a phone call to review what is best for you.

Consider many options when deciding which Internet service(s) would be best for you. The quality of RV internet service can be affected by various conditions, including (but not in any particular order):

1. Speed: Consider how much bandwidth you need for online activities. This could include browsing, streaming, gaming, or downloading/ uploading large files. Choose a plan with sufficient download and upload speeds to accommodate your usage requirements. It is easy to find your speed on any internet connection. Just log into the free service **www.fast.com**[1]. The average speed should be around 100mps (minimum 25mps) download and 10mps upload.

2. Connection Type: Different types of internet connections are available, including DSL, cable, fiber-optic, satellite, and fixed wireless. Each class has advantages and limitations regarding speed, availability, cost, and reliability. Choose the one that best suits your location and budget.

3. Reliability: Look for an internet service provider (ISP) with a reputation for reliability and minimal downtime. Check customer reviews and ratings to gauge the reliability of the service in your area.

4. Availability: Only some types of internet connections are available in some locations. If you travel quite a bit, your needs will differ from those who stay in a park for long periods. Check with local ISPs to see which options are available in your area and whether they can service your

---

1. https://d.docs.live.net/edd1f4cb0a829972/Documents/www.fast.com

address. For example, major carriers are not allowed to provide service in our park since the park has an agreement with an outside park service. When you ask the major carriers for your address, the service says they cannot connect.

5. Cost: Compare the costs of different internet plans, including monthly fees, installation fees, equipment rental fees, and any additional charges. Consider any promotional offers or discounts that may be available for new customers. You will find a vast difference between costs,

6. Data Caps: Some internet plans may have data caps or limits on monthly data usage. Many services now claim that they give you unlimited data usage, but in the fine print, they say they significantly slow your service down after so many gigabytes are used. As stated in the contract, the one I use is not allowed to do that. Finding my service took me a while, but they are out there. Consider whether these limitations affect your usage patterns and whether you need an unlimited data plan.

7. Customer Support: Consider the ISP's quality of customer support. Look for reviews and testimonials from existing customers to gauge the responsiveness and helpfulness of customer support representatives. I stick with national companies and find that I rarely ever need to contact customer service, but it should be a consideration.

8. Additional Features: Some ISPs offer bundled services (e.g., TV or phone), free Wi-Fi hotspot access, security features, or cloud storage. Consider whether these additional features are valuable to you.

9. Contract Terms: Pay attention to the terms of service and contract length. Some ISPs may require a long-term contract, while others offer month-to-month or no-contract options. Be aware of any early termination fees or penalties for canceling service before the contract ends.

10. Future Expansion: Consider your future needs for internet connectivity. Will you need to upgrade your plan or add additional services as your usage patterns change? Choose an ISP that can accommodate your future needs.

11. Location: The availability and quality of internet service can vary significantly depending on where the RV is parked or traveling. Rural areas may have limited coverage or slower internet speeds than urban

areas. Boondocking, staying at one site all the time, or traveling to many different parks could all mean another type of service is needed. Physical obstacles such as mountains, hills, and dense foliage can obstruct cellular signals, weakening internet connectivity in certain areas.

12. Cellular Coverage: Many RV users use cellular data for internet connectivity. The quality of cellular coverage, including signal strength and network congestion, directly impacts the quality of internet service. View Appendix N for cellular coverage maps of the major carriers.

13. Terrain: Mountains and valleys can significantly contribute to poor reception from cell towers.

14. Weather Conditions: Extreme weather conditions like heavy rain, snow, or storms can interfere with cellular signals and degrade internet service quality.

15. Network Congestion: During peak hours or in densely populated areas, cellular networks may experience congestion, resulting in slower internet speeds and reduced reliability. In our park, users of the park internet system share much congestion during early evening hours and firm seasonal peaks—when you want it!

16. Proximity to Cell Towers: The distance between the RV and the nearest cell tower affects signal strength and internet service quality. RVs parked farther away from cell towers may experience weaker signals and slower speeds. You can use the Open Signal Free app (iPhone or Android) to review where coverage is. They also offer a premium version if you see value in that.

17. Type of Antenna and Equipment: The type and quality of antennas, signal boosters, and other equipment used to enhance internet connectivity in the RV can significantly impact service quality.

18. Service Provider: Different cellular service providers offer varying coverage areas, network technologies, and data plans, which can affect the overall quality of internet service available to RV users.

19. Interference: Electrical interference from nearby devices or appliances within the RV can potentially disrupt cellular signals and impact internet service quality.

20. Data Plan and Throttling: Some cellular data plans may impose data

caps or throttle internet speeds after reaching certain usage thresholds, affecting RV users' internet service quality.

21. Satellite Internet: RVs with satellite internet systems may experience service interruptions or degraded performance due to line-of-sight obstructions, inclement weather, and equipment malfunctions.

22. Number of Connections Needed: Some services allow one item to be connected simultaneously (like my cell phone hotspot). My home internet system allows up to 40 items! I have my phone, computer, Kindle, three TVs, virtual headset, watch, and three Amazon Alexa's all connected and have never run into a problem. It would not be unusual for five or six items to run simultaneously.

23. Backup: You may find that your system goes down sometimes (they all do at some point!) and that you can't afford it to stop working. In such situations, having a backup on a different system would be necessary. I use my phone's Hotspot as a backup.

Considering these factors, RV travelers should be prepared to adapt to varying conditions and explore alternative internet connectivity options to ensure a reliable internet connection while on the road. It may be necessary for you to have several different options, as I do. I use my business account connection (which can also be used for personal accounts!) and my phone's Hotspot. That way, I have two different networks (in case of a problem with one). Please get in touch with me if you want to know the specifics of what I use. I try not to promote companies in my writings.

Use the form on the next page to mark what is essential for you. We will briefly cover the pros and cons of each service, and you can then compare them to your needs. That should help you discover the best method(s) for you.

Use the form below to determine what is important to you. Place a checkmark next to the items that are very important to you. If it would help, prioritize them on a scale of 1 to 5, with one being the most important. Contact me if you need any assistance. There is a copy of this form on our website if you would like to print it off.

1	Speed	__________
2	Connection Type	__________
3	Reliability	__________
4	Availability	__________
5	Cost	__________
6	Data Caps	__________
7	Customer Support	__________
8	Additional Features	__________
9	Contract Terms	__________
10	Future Expansion	__________
11	Location	__________
12	Cellular Coverage	__________
13	Terrain	__________
14	Weather Conditions	__________
15	Network Congestion	__________
16	Proximity to Cell Towers	__________
17	Type of Antenna and Equipment	__________
18	Service Provider	__________
19	Interference	__________
20	Data Plan and Throttling	__________
21	Satellite Internet	__________
22	Number of Connections Needed	__________
23	Backup Necessary	__________
24		__________
25		__________

What is Important to You?

Chapter 5

Types of RV Internet Connections

RVers can access various internet connection options with advantages, disadvantages, and considerations. This chapter analyzes the different types of RV internet connections, empowering readers to choose the most suitable option based on their needs, travel preferences, and budget.

5.1 Cellular Data

Cellular data is one of the most popular and widely available internet connection options for RVers. Utilizing the cellular networks of major carriers such as Verizon, AT&T, and T-Mobile, RVers can access high-speed internet on the go. Cellular data plans come in various tiers, offering different data allowances, speeds, and coverage areas. RVers can use smartphones, mobile hotspots, or dedicated cellular routers to access cellular data and create a Wi-Fi network for their devices.

Advantages:

- Wide coverage across urban, suburban, and rural areas. You're not tied to a specific location like you would be with Wi-Fi
- High-speed internet access for streaming, gaming, and remote work
- Flexibility to choose from a variety of data plans and carriers
- No additional hardware or equipment is required for basic connectivity. No Dependency on Wi-Fi Networks: Cellular data occurs when Wi-Fi is unavailable or reliable. Your mobile data keeps you online on a road trip, at a park, or in transit
- Urgent or Critical Tasks: Cellular data ensures you have internet access for essential tasks that can't wait. It's handy during emergencies or when you need to access information promptly

Disadvantages:

- Limited coverage in remote and wilderness areas with poor cellular reception

- Potential data caps, throttling, and overage charges on unlimited plans
- Dependent on the availability and reliability of cellular networks in specific locations

- Requires a compatible device with cellular capabilities and a data plan from a carrier
- Data Costs: Cellular data plans can be expensive, significantly, if you exceed your data limits. Streaming videos, gaming, or downloading large files can quickly affect your data allowance

5.2 Satellite Internet

Satellite internet offers RVers reliable connectivity in remote and off-grid locations where traditional cellular networks may be unavailable. By leveraging satellites orbiting the Earth, satellite internet providers deliver broadband internet access to RVers across the globe. RVers can install satellite dishes and modems on their RVs to establish a connection with the satellite network, enabling them to access the internet from virtually anywhere.

Advantages:

- Global coverage in even the most remote and isolated areas. Availability in Rural Areas: Cellular service is unavailable or spotty in many rural areas. Satellite internet is for those residing in less populated or rural regions where other internet options are inaccessible.
- Relatively high-speed internet access for browsing, email, and basic activities
- Independence from terrestrial infrastructure, making it suitable for off-grid living
- Consistent performance unaffected by terrain, weather, or local infrastructure

- No Cable Wiring Delays: With satellite internet, you won't have to depend on any wiring or service from your campground. The signal is beamed directly from space to your RV

Disadvantages:

- There are high upfront costs for equipment purchase, installation, and setup. Monthly fees can also be increased
- Limited bandwidth and data allowances compared to terrestrial internet options
- Latency: Satellite internet involves a longer round-trip time for data between your device and the orbiting satellite. This latency can impact real-time applications like video calls or online gaming
- Susceptibility to signal interference from weather conditions, foliage, and obstructions

5.3 Wi-Fi Hotspots

Wi-Fi hotspots provide RVers with convenient and cost-effective internet access in urban and suburban areas with Wi-Fi coverage. RVers can connect to Wi-Fi networks offered by cafes, restaurants, libraries, RV parks, and other public spaces to access the internet on their devices. Additionally, some RV parks and campgrounds offer Wi-Fi access to guests, allowing RVers to stay connected while parked at their destination.

Advantages:

- Cost-effective solution for internet access in urban and suburban areas
- Convenient access to Wi-Fi networks in public spaces and RV parks
- No additional equipment or subscription fees required for basic connectivity
- Allows RVers to conserve cellular data and minimize usage
- You can use your phone as a hotspot without carrying an additional device, many times at no extra costs.[11]

Disadvantages:

- Limited coverage and availability in rural and remote areas with sparse Wi-Fi infrastructure
- Shared network bandwidth leading to slow speeds and congestion during peak hours
- Security risks associated with public Wi-Fi networks, including data

---

1. https://www.switchful.com/service/internet/resource/what-is-a-hotspot

privacy and hacking threats

- Reliance on external Wi-Fi sources, making it unsuitable for off-grid or wilderness camping
- Limited Data: Hotspot data is subject to restrictions. Cellular companies impose stricter limits due to network capacity. You won't get unlimited hotspot data, often at a higher price per gigabyte
- Speed Variability: Cellular data speeds don't match those of fiber or cable internet. While 5G home internet is improving, you may still experience fluctuating rates and occasional outages

5.4 Campground Wi-Fi

Many RV parks and campgrounds offer guests Wi-Fi access as part of their amenities and services. RVers can connect to campground Wi-Fi networks using their devices to access the internet while staying there. Campground Wi-Fi networks vary in speed, reliability, and coverage, depending on the location, infrastructure, and provider.

Advantages:

- Included as part of campground amenities, often at no additional cost to guests
- Allows RVers to access the internet while parked at the campground
- May offer faster speeds and more reliable connectivity than public Wi-Fi networks
- Convenient for staying connected with fellow campers and accessing campground services

Disadvantages:

- Variable quality and reliability of campground Wi-Fi networks, depending on location and provider
- Limited coverage and signal strength, particularly in remote and rural areas with limited infrastructure
- Shared network bandwidth leading to congestion and slow speeds during peak usage times
- May require additional equipment such as Wi-Fi extenders or antennas

for improved connectivity

- Signal Strength and Speed: The signal strength diminishes the further away you are from the source. Your connectivity might be spotty if your tent is set up farther away. Additionally, the speed may not be optimal, similar to Wi-Fi at a busy coffee shop

Chapter 6

So What's Best for You?

This is the chapter you should look back at several times! Filling out this form should tell you what service(s) would be best for you. I suggest you continue reading the remaining chapters to better understand the industry, then return and complete this form.

These are the primary categories you should consider when deciding what type of service to purchase. When researching, complete these fields and determine which are most important.

1-5 scale, 5 being highly important

	Satellite	Cellular	Hotspot	Campgrd Wi-Fi
Speed	______	______	______	______
Availability	______	______	______	______
Cost	______	______	______	______
Data Caps	______	______	______	______
Location	______	______	______	______
Terrain	______	______	______	______
Weather Conditions	______	______	______	______
Network Congestion	______	______	______	______
Proximity to Cell Towers	______	______	______	______

Chapter 7

Differences Between 5G and 2.4

5G and 2.4 GHz refer to different generations and frequencies of wireless communication technologies commonly used for mobile and Wi-Fi networks. Your devices may or may not be available. Here's a comparison between them:

7.1 Generation

5G: 5G stands for "fifth generation" and represents the latest standard in mobile network technology. It offers significant speed, capacity, and latency improvements over previous generations (such as 4G LTE).

2.4 GHz: 2.4 GHz refers to the frequency band used by Wi-Fi networks. It's part of the IEEE 802.11 wireless networking standard and has been used for Wi-Fi communication for several generations, including 802.11b, 802.11g, and 802.11n.

7.2 Lower and Higher Frequency

5G: 5G operates across a range of frequencies, including both lower frequencies (sub-6 GHz) and higher frequencies (mmWave). Sub-1. GHz frequencies provide broader coverage and better penetration through obstacles, while mmWave frequencies offer faster speeds but have a shorter range and limited indoor penetration.

2.4 GHz: Wi-Fi networks operating in the 2.4 GHz frequency band use a single frequency channel within the 2.4 GHz range. This frequency band is prone to interference from other devices (such as Bluetooth, microwaves, and cordless phones) and has limited capacity compared to higher frequency bands.

7.3 Speed and Capacity

5G: 5G networks offer significantly faster download and upload speeds than previous generations of mobile networks. They also have much greater capacity, simultaneously enabling support for many devices and facilitating bandwidth-intensive applications such as 4K video streaming and virtual reality.

2.4 GHz: Wi-Fi networks operating in the 2.4 GHz band typically offer lower speeds and capacity than 5G networks. While adequate for basic internet browsing and streaming, 2.4 GHz Wi-Fi may need help to deliver consistent performance in crowded environments with many connected devices.

7.4 Understanding When to Use

5G: 5G technology enables various applications, including enhanced mobile broadband, connectivity, autonomous vehicles, remote healthcare, and industrial automation.

2.4 GHz: Wi-Fi networks operating in the 2.4 GHz band are commonly used for RV and office internet access and wireless networking for devices such as smartphones, laptops, tablets, and intelligent RV devices.

Chapter 8

Enhancing RV Internet Performance

Optimizing RV internet performance is essential for ensuring seamless connectivity and a smooth online experience while on the road. This chapter explores various strategies, technologies, and best practices for enhancing RV internet performance, empowering RVers to stay connected wherever their adventures occur.

8.1 Signal Boosters and Amplifiers

Signal boosters and amplifiers improve cellular signal strength and reception in weak or unreliable coverage areas. These devices capture existing cellular signals, amplify them, and rebroadcast them within the RV, resulting in more robust and consistent connections. RVers can choose from various signal boosters and amplifiers for frequency bands and network technologies.

8.2 Antennas and External Equipment

Installing external antennas on the RV can significantly enhance internet connectivity by maximizing signal reception and minimizing interference. Directional antennas, omnidirectional antennas, and satellite dishes are famous for RVers seeking to improve their internet performance. Additionally, installing rooftop mounts, pole mounts, or mast extensions can elevate antennas and optimize their line-of-sight with cellular towers and satellite satellites, further improving signal quality.

8.3 Cellular Routers and Hotspots

Cellular routers and hotspots are dedicated devices designed to create Wi-Fi networks using cellular data connections. These devices offer advanced features such as multiple SIM card slots, load balancing, and failover capabilities, ensuring reliable and high-speed internet access for various devices. RVers can connect smartphones, tablets, laptops, smart TVs, and machines to cellular routers and hotspots, creating a comprehensive internet ecosystem within the RV.

8.4 Data Management Tools and Applications

Managing data usage is essential for optimizing RV internet performance and avoiding overage charges or throttling. Data management tools and applications allow RVers to monitor their data usage in real time, set data usage alerts and limits, and prioritize data-intensive activities. Additionally, data compression techniques, ad blockers, and content caching solutions can help reduce data consumption and improve internet speed and responsiveness.

8.5 Wi-Fi Extenders and Repeaters

Wi-Fi extenders and repeaters are valuable devices for extending the range and coverage of existing Wi-Fi networks in RV parks, campgrounds, and other public spaces. These devices capture Wi-Fi signals from distant access points, amplify them, and rebroadcast them within the RV, improving connectivity and signal strength. RVers can strategically install Wi-Fi extenders and repeaters to cover dead zones and eliminate Wi-Fi dead spots within their RVs.

Wi-Fi extenders and Wi-Fi repeaters are both devices used to extend the coverage range of a wireless network, but they accomplish this in slightly different ways.

1. Wi-Fi Extender: A Wi-Fi extender, also known as a range extender or booster, works by receiving the existing Wi-Fi signal from your router and then rebroadcasting it to areas of your RV or office where the signal is weak or nonexistent. Essentially, it acts as a bridge between your router and your devices, extending the coverage area of your Wi-Fi network without sacrificing performance. Wi-Fi extenders typically wirelessly connect to your existing Wi-Fi network or via an Ethernet cable.

2. Wi-Fi Repeater: A Wi-Fi repeater, on the other hand, works by receiving the existing Wi-Fi signal from your router, amplifying it, and then rebroadcasting it to extend the coverage area. Unlike a Wi-Fi extender, a repeater must be placed within range of your router's signal and the location where you want to improve coverage. The repeater then creates a new network with its own SSID (network name) and password, essentially repeating the signal from your router. Devices connect to the repeater's network rather than directly to your router.

In summary, the main difference between a Wi-Fi extender and a Wi-Fi repeater is how they handle the existing Wi-Fi signal. An extender rebroadcasts the original signal, while a repeater amplifies and then rebroadcasts it as a new signal. Both devices serve the same purpose of extending Wi-Fi coverage, but they may be more suitable for different scenarios depending on your specific needs and network setup.

8.6 Mesh Networking Systems

Mesh networking systems offer seamless and reliable Wi-Fi coverage throughout the RV by creating a network of interconnected access points. These systems utilize multiple access points placed strategically within the RV to provide blanket coverage and eliminate Wi-Fi dead spots. Mesh networking systems offer seamless roaming, self-healing capabilities, and centralized management, making them ideal for RVers seeking comprehensive Wi-Fi coverage and performance.

8.7 Off-Grid Connectivity Solutions

For RVers venturing off-grid or camping in remote wilderness areas, off-grid connectivity solutions are essential for maintaining internet access. Solar-powered cellular routers, satellite internet systems, and long-range Wi-Fi antennas are off-grid connectivity solutions that enable RVers to stay connected even in the most remote and isolated locations. These solutions provide peace of mind and security for RVers exploring off-the-beaten-path destinations.

Chapter 9

RV Internet Security and Privacy

In an increasingly connected world, ensuring the security and privacy of RV internet connections is paramount. This chapter explores best practices, tools, and technologies for safeguarding sensitive data and protecting RVers from cyber threats while enjoying internet connectivity on the road.

9.1 Encryption Protocols and Secure Connections

Utilizing encryption protocols such as WPA2 (Wi-Fi Protected Access 2) and HTTPS (Hypertext Transfer Protocol Secure) helps secure internet connections and protect data transmitted between devices and servers. RVers should ensure that their Wi-Fi networks, cellular connections, and online accounts are configured to use encryption whenever possible to prevent eavesdropping and data interception by malicious actors.

9.2 Virtual Private Networks (VPNs)

Virtual Private Networks (VPNs) are powerful tools for enhancing online privacy and security by encrypting internet traffic and routing it through secure servers. RVers can use VPNs to establish secure connections and mask their IP addresses, making it difficult for third parties to track their online activities or intercept sensitive information. VPNs are beneficial when accessing public Wi-Fi networks or conducting sensitive transactions online.

9.3 Firewall Settings and Network Security

Configuring firewall settings on routers, devices, and operating systems helps prevent unauthorized access to RV networks and devices. Firewalls act as barriers between trusted and untrusted networks, filtering incoming and outgoing traffic based on predefined rules and policies. RVers should regularly update firewall settings, enable intrusion detection systems, and monitor network traffic for signs of suspicious activity to maintain a secure and protected online environment.

9.4 Secure Browsing Habits

Practicing secure browsing habits is essential for protecting against online threats such as malware, phishing, and identity theft. RVers should be cautious when clicking links, downloading files, and sharing personal information online.

They should also keep their devices and software up to date with the latest security patches and updates to mitigate vulnerabilities and exploits that cybercriminals could exploit.

You must understand the difference between HTTP and HTTPS. Look at the link that just connected you to an Internet site. Does it show HTTP or HTTPS at the beginning?

The differences between HTTP and HTTPS lie in their security:

1. HTTP (Hypertext Transfer Protocol):
    - HTTP is a protocol used for transferring data over the internet.
    - It operates over TCP/IP and is the foundation of data communication on the World Wide Web.
    - HTTP data is sent in plain text, making it susceptible to interception and eavesdropping by malicious actors.
    - It does not provide any encryption or data integrity mechanisms.
2. HTTPS (Hypertext Transfer Protocol Secure):
    - HTTPS is an extension of HTTP that adds a layer of security through encryption and authentication.
    - It uses SSL/TLS (Secure Sockets Layer/Transport Layer Security) to encrypt data before transmission, providing confidentiality and preventing eavesdropping.
    - HTTPS ensures data integrity by verifying that it has not been tampered with during transmission.
    - It uses digital certificates to authenticate the website's identity, helping users verify that they connect to the intended destination, not an impostor.
    - Websites using HTTPS display a padlock icon in the address bar of web browsers, indicating a secure connection.

In summary, while HTTP and HTTPS are protocols for transferring data over the internet, HTTPS provides an additional layer of security through encryption and authentication, making transmitting sensitive information such as login credentials, financial data, and personal information safer. It's essential for protecting data privacy and preventing unauthorized access or tampering. If you exchange ANY personal information on a website, ensure HTTPS shows.

9.5 Two-Factor Authentication (2FA)

Enabling Two-Factor Authentication (2FA) adds an extra layer of security to online accounts by requiring users to provide two forms of authentication, typically a password and a one-time code sent to their mobile device. RVers should enable 2FA whenever possible for their email accounts, banking accounts, social media profiles, and other online services to prevent unauthorized access and protect their sensitive information from being compromised.

9.6 Secure Data Storage and Backup

Securing and backing up data is essential for protecting against data loss due to theft, hardware failure, or cyber-attacks. RVers should encrypt sensitive data stored on their devices and use secure cloud storage services with robust encryption and authentication mechanisms. Regularly backing up data to external hard drives, USB drives, or cloud storage ensures that valuable information remains safe and accessible during unforeseen circumstances.

9.7 Privacy-Focused Browsers and Tools

Using privacy-focused browsers such as Brave, Firefox, or DuckDuckGo and privacy-enhancing browser extensions such as uBlock Origin, HTTPS Everywhere, and Privacy Badger helps minimize online tracking and data collection by advertisers and third-party trackers. RVers should configure their browsers to block cookies, track scripts, and intrusive advertisements to preserve their online privacy and anonymity while browsing the web.

Chapter 10

Tips for Maximizing RV Internet Experience

In the fast-paced world of RVing, having a reliable and efficient internet connection can significantly enhance the overall experience on the road. This chapter offers practical tips, strategies, and recommendations for RVers to maximize their internet experience, ensuring seamless connectivity and enjoyment during their travels.

10.1 Choose the Right Data Plan

Selecting the right data plan is crucial for RVers to ensure sufficient data allowance and optimal connectivity on the road. When choosing a data plan from cellular providers, consider data usage habits, coverage areas, network speeds, and pricing. Evaluate options for unlimited data plans, shared family plans, or pay-as-you-go plans based on your individual needs and budget.

10.2 Utilize Signal Boosters and Antennas

Investing in signal boosters and antennas can significantly improve cellular reception and internet performance in areas with weak or spotty coverage. Install external antennas and signal boosters on your RV to maximize signal strength and minimize interference from surrounding obstacles. Position antennas strategically to align with cellular towers and satellite satellites for optimal signal reception.

10.3 Manage Data Usage Wisely

Managing data usage effectively is essential for avoiding overage charges and maximizing available data allowances. Monitor data usage regularly using built-in data tracking tools or third-party apps to stay within your plan limits. Prioritize essential activities such as work-related tasks, navigation, and communication, and limit bandwidth-intensive activities like streaming and downloading large files.

All smartphones and most Internet services have a way to track data usage. Be sure to follow the rules of your data plans. My data plan does not have a usage limit, but my phone does. After a certain amount of data usage, it slows down, which is always at a critical time!

10.4 Secure Your Wi-Fi Network

Securing your Wi-Fi network is essential for protecting against unauthorized access and maintaining privacy while connected to the internet. Change default passwords, enable encryption protocols, and configure firewall settings on your router to safeguard your network from potential threats and intrusions. Consider using Virtual Private Networks (VPNs) for additional encryption and anonymity when accessing public Wi-Fi networks.

10.5 Optimize Device Settings and Updates

Optimizing device settings and keeping software up to date is crucial for maintaining optimal internet performance and security. Enable automatic software updates on your devices to ensure they receive the latest bug fixes, security patches, and performance enhancements. Configure device settings to prioritize Wi-Fi networks, reduce background data usage, and limit app permissions to conserve data and battery life.

10.6 Explore Off-Grid Connectivity Solutions

Exploring off-grid connectivity solutions can provide peace of mind and security for RVers venturing into remote and wilderness areas. Invest in solar-powered cellular routers, satellite internet systems, or long-range Wi-Fi antennas to maintain internet access even in areas with limited infrastructure: plan and research off-grid campsites and boondocking locations with available connectivity options.

10.7 Backup and Secure Your Data

Backing up and securing your data is essential for protecting valuable information and ensuring continuity in the event of hardware failure or loss. Use cloud storage services, external hard drives, or USB drives to regularly back up important files, documents, and media. Encrypt sensitive data and enable security features such as remote wipe and device tracking to prevent unauthorized access and data breaches.

10.8 Stay Informed and Adapt

Staying informed about new technologies, trends, and developments in RV internet technology is essential for adapting to evolving connectivity needs and challenges. Join online forums, social media groups, and RVing communities to share experiences, exchange tips, and learn from fellow RVers. Keep abreast of industry news, product reviews, and expert recommendations to make informed decisions about your RV internet setup. As long as there is interest, I will update this eBook every six months and provide you with a free update as long as I have your email address. Read the end of the eBook for further information.

RV Weight Management: Stay within your RV's weight limits by distributing cargo evenly and avoiding overloading. Use weighing scales to measure axle weights and adjust your load to maintain safe towing or driving conditions. Most of us do not realize how much weight we carry and how we may have moved the RV out of balance. Any significant changes, inside or out, should encourage us to check the weight!

Chapter 11

Future Trends in RV Internet Technology

The world of RV internet technology is dynamic and ever-evolving, with continuous innovations and advancements shaping the future of connectivity on the road. This chapter explores emerging trends, cutting-edge technologies, and future developments in RV internet technology, providing insights into the exciting possibilities for RVers.

11.1 5G Connectivity

The rollout of 5G networks promises to revolutionize RV internet connectivity by delivering faster speeds, lower latency, and greater bandwidth capacity than ever before. 5G technology enables RVers to enjoy ultra-high-definition streaming, real-time gaming, and seamless video conferencing. As 5G networks expand and mature, RVers can expect enhanced internet performance and reliability in urban, suburban, and rural areas.

11.2 Integration

Integrating smart devices and innovative technology into RVs enables unprecedented road automation, control, and connectivity. Smart RVs with connected appliances, thermostats, security systems, and entertainment devices offer enhanced comfort, convenience, and efficiency for RVers. Sensors and monitoring systems provide real-time data on RV systems and environmental conditions, improving safety and peace of mind while traveling.

11.3 Artificial Intelligence (AI) and Machine Learning

Artificial Intelligence (AI) and machine learning technologies have the potential to revolutionize RV internet technology by enabling personalized experiences, predictive analytics, and autonomous capabilities. AI-powered assistants and virtual companions offer customized recommendations, travel insights, and itinerary suggestions tailored to individual preferences and interests. Machine learning algorithms optimize internet performance, predict user behavior, and adapt to changing network conditions, ensuring seamless connectivity and user experience on the road.

11.4 Augmented Reality (AR) and Virtual Reality (VR)

Augmented Reality (AR) and Virtual Reality (VR) technologies offer immersive and interactive experiences for RVers, enhancing entertainment, education, and exploration on the road. AR navigation systems overlay real-time information and points of interest onto the RV windshield, providing intuitive directions and enhanced situational awareness while driving. VR travel experiences transport RVers to distant destinations, historical landmarks, and natural wonders, allowing them to explore and discover new places from the comfort of their RVs.

11.5 Smart Infrastructure and Connected Campgrounds

Intelligent infrastructure development and connected campgrounds enable RVers to enjoy enhanced amenities, services, and experiences while staying at RV parks and campgrounds. Innovative RV parks equipped with Wi-Fi access, electric vehicle charging stations, waste management systems, and automated check-in processes offer convenience and comfort for RVers. Connected campgrounds provide real-time updates on availability, pricing, and amenities, enabling RVers to plan and book their stays easily.

11.6 Sustainable and Eco-Friendly Solutions

Adopting sustainable and eco-friendly solutions in RV internet technology reflects a growing emphasis on environmental conservation and responsible travel practices. Solar-powered cellular routers, energy-efficient devices, and eco-friendly materials reduce carbon footprint and minimize environmental impact while traveling on the road. RVers can embrace sustainable living and eco-consciousness by incorporating green technologies and practices into their RV internet setups.

Chapter 12

Case Studies and Success Stories

Real-life examples and success stories illustrate how RVers leverage internet technology to enhance their travel experiences. This chapter features case studies of RVers who have overcome connectivity challenges, achieved remote work-life balance, and embraced the freedom of RV living with the help of advanced internet solutions.

12.1 Case Study: The Digital Nomad Family

Meet the Johnson family, digital nomads traveling full-time in their RV for the past two years. With two young children and remote jobs in web development and online marketing, staying connected on the road is essential for the Johnsons. They rely on cellular data, Wi-Fi hotspots, and a powerful cellular router to maintain internet access wherever their adventures take them. By embracing a nomadic lifestyle and leveraging technology to work and learn remotely, the Johnsons have created unforgettable memories and experiences for their family while exploring the country.

12.2 Case Study: The Adventure Photographer

Jake, an adventure photographer and outdoor enthusiast, spends months traveling solo in his RV to capture stunning landscapes and wildlife in remote locations. Reliable internet connectivity is crucial for Jake to share his photography portfolio, communicate with clients, and upload content to social media platforms. Equipped with a satellite internet system and solar-powered setup, Jake can stay connected and pursue his passion for photography while immersing himself in the beauty of nature.

12.3 Case Study: The Retired Couple

After retiring and downsizing to an RV, Jim and Diane embarked on a cross-country road trip to explore national parks and scenic destinations. While they cherish the freedom of RV living, staying connected with friends and family back in the RV is essential to them. Jim and Diane utilize campground Wi-Fi and cellular data to keep in touch, share travel updates, and research their next destination. By embracing technology and connectivity, they can enjoy their retirement years while staying connected with loved ones.

12.4 Case Study: The Remote Worker

Sarah, a marketing consultant and remote worker, travels part-time in her RV while managing her business remotely. Reliable internet access is critical for Sarah to attend virtual meetings, collaborate with clients, and access cloud-based tools and resources. She relies on cellular data, Wi-Fi hotspots, and a VPN for secure connectivity on the road. By embracing the remote work lifestyle and leveraging technology to stay productive, Sarah enjoys the flexibility and freedom of RV travel without sacrificing her career goals.

12.5 Case Study: The Full-Time RVer

Mark and Lisa, a retired couple, sold their house and embarked on a full-time RV adventure to explore North America. While they enjoy the freedom and spontaneity of RV living, staying connected with their grandchildren is their top priority. Mark and Lisa utilize a satellite internet system and video calling apps to keep in touch with their family members and share their travel experiences in real time. By embracing technology, they can maintain strong family bonds and create lasting memories despite being thousands of miles away from RV.

Conclusion

I hope this eBook provided enough information to help you choose the most beneficial Internet service(s) and help you understand the pieces that will allow you to decide if you need to make any changes.

I started using the Internet in 1985 when I set up my first website. I remember hearing the noise on the phone line when the computer connected. It has come a long way since then! What I have today is not what I used when I first started RVing, and it probably won't be the same as what I will use in five years. I enjoy the challenge of constantly looking for more options and staying abreast of market changes.

I plan to update this eBook every six months if there is interest. For a free update, please visit my website, **www.FreeLiving.com**[1], and enter your name and email address. I will cross-reference it with your original purchase and send you a link to download the new eBook.

I would gladly respond to your email or phone call if you have questions or want guidance on the best system. I don't share the specific product names used in this eBook because I prefer that readers make informed decisions and don't get influenced by people quietly receiving affiliate compensation. I would be glad to share them in any one-on-one discussion. You may contact me at info@FancyFreeLiving.com

Thank you for your eBook purchase.

Fancy Free Living, LLC
7901 4th St N STE 300
St. Petersburg, FL 33702
(352) 234-8277
info@FancyFreeLiving.com
www.FreeLiving.com[2]

APPENDIX

---

1.   https://d.docs.live.net/edd1f4cb0a829972/Documents/www.FreeLiving.com

2. https://d.docs.live.net/edd1f4cb0a829972/Documents/www.FreeLiving.com

Appendix A

Basic Definitions

4G (Fourth Generation): Provides high-speed download and upload packets of information. It is the most common today, with 4G making substantial advances over it.

5G (Fifth Generation) offers faster speeds and higher bandwidth than 4G. It incorporates new technology and uses a higher radio frequency than 4G.

Bandwidth: The amount of data transferable over a given period.

Bit: The smallest unit of data in a computer. Data sizes start at Kilobytes (1,024 bits), Megabytes (8 million bits), Gigabytes (8 billion bits), and Terabytes (8 trillion bits). They do go higher, but they are seldom used in regular discussions.

Cellular Data Definitions

A cellular data connection, often called "cellular data," is a wireless connection that allows mobile devices to access the internet using cellular networks. These networks are operated by telecommunications companies (such as AT&T, Verizon, T-Mobile, etc.) and use a system of cell towers to provide coverage over a wide geographic area.

An extender- also known as a Range Extender—is a device that amplifies and extends the coverage area of a wireless network, improving signal strength in areas with weak connectivity.

IP Address: A unique identifier for a specific computer or device on a network. All of our devices have their IP address.

Router

A router is a networking device that forwards data packets between computer networks. It is a central hub for connecting multiple devices to a local area network (LAN) and facilitates communication between the devices and the Internet.

Appendix B

Hotspots- All the Information You Need

A hotspot is a physical location where people can access the internet using Wi-Fi technology. It's typically created using a "hotspot" or "mobile hotspot," often a smartphone, tablet, or dedicated portable hotspot device. When activated, the hotspot device creates a Wi-Fi network that other devices, such as laptops, smartphones, or tablets, can access for internet access.

Here's how it generally works:

1. Device Configuration: The owner of the hotspot-enabled device (e.g., smartphone) activates the hotspot feature in the device's settings. They may also set a network name (SSID) and password for security.
2. Wireless Network Creation: Once activated, the device broadcasts a Wi-Fi signal, creating a small local area network (LAN) around itself.
3. Connection: Other devices within the Wi-Fi signal range can detect and connect to the hotspot network. Users typically need to enter the SSID and password to establish a connection.
4. Internet Access: Once connected, devices can access the Internet through the hotspot-enabled device's cellular data connection. The hotspot device acts as a bridge, allowing connected devices to access the Internet via the cellular network.
5. Data Usage: Data consumed by devices connected to the hotspot is typically counted against the hotspot-enabled device's data plan. Users should be mindful of their data usage to avoid exceeding their limits and incurring additional charges.

Hotspots are commonly used when traditional wired or Wi-Fi internet access is unavailable or inconvenient, such as when traveling, in public spaces, or in emergencies. They provide a convenient way for multiple devices to share a single internet connection, offering flexibility and connectivity on the go. However, users should be aware of security risks associated with public Wi-Fi networks and take appropriate measures to protect their data and privacy when using hotspots.

A hotspot is a physical location where people can access the internet using Wi-Fi technology. It's an area where wireless internet access is available to devices with Wi-Fi capability, such as smartphones, laptops, tablets, or other wireless-enabled devices.

Hotspots can be found in various public places, such as cafes, airports, libraries, hotels, restaurants, and outdoor areas like parks or city squares. Businesses, institutions, or municipalities can provide them to offer internet connectivity to their customers, visitors, or residents.

Hotspots offer a convenient way to get online when they're away from the RV or the office. They're handy for travelers, remote workers, students, and anyone who needs temporary internet access while on the go. However, users should be aware of security risks associated with public Wi-Fi networks and take appropriate measures to protect their devices and data when using hotspots.

Appendix C

Understanding Throttling

Throttling, in the context of internet usage, refers to intentionally slowing down or restricting internet speed by an internet service provider (ISP) or network operator. Throttling can occur for various reasons and affect different types of internet connections, including wired broadband, cellular data, and even certain types of applications or services.

Here are some common reasons why throttling might occur:

1. Network Management: ISPs may throttle internet speeds during network congestion to ensure all users have fair access to available bandwidth. By reducing the rate for all users, ISPs can prevent certain users or applications from monopolizing the available bandwidth and degrading the experience for others.

2. Data Caps: Some ISPs impose data caps or limits on how much data users can consume within a certain period (e.g., monthly). If users exceed these limits, their internet speeds may be throttled until the start of the next billing cycle.

3. Traffic Shaping: ISPs may throttle specific types of internet traffic or applications to manage network traffic more effectively. For example, during peak usage hours, they might prioritize certain types of traffic (such as web browsing or email) over others (such as peer-to-peer file sharing or video streaming).

4. Contract Violations: ISPs may throttle internet speeds for users who violate their terms of service or acceptable use policies. This could include activities such as illegal downloading or excessive use of network resources.

Throttling can have significant implications for users, resulting in slower internet speeds, reduced performance for specific applications or services, and a less satisfactory online experience overall. Users who believe that their internet speeds are being throttled unfairly can often contact their ISP for clarification or explore alternative options for internet service. Additionally, regulatory bodies in some regions may impose rules or guidelines to limit or regulate ISPs' throttling practices.

Appendix D

Verizon Versus Starlink Comparison

Verizon and Starlink are two data network suppliers offering distinct services and technologies. Here's a comparison of some key differences between them:

1. Technology:
    - Verizon: Verizon is a traditional telecommunications company primarily offering cellular data services. It operates a nationwide cellular network infrastructure consisting of cell towers and supporting infrastructure to provide its customers with wireless voice and data services.
    - Starlink: SpaceX, Elon Musk's aerospace company, provides Starlink, a satellite internet service. It utilizes a constellation of low-earth orbit (LEO) satellites to provide broadband internet access to users worldwide, particularly in underserved or remote areas where traditional wired or cellular internet infrastructure may be lacking.

1. Coverage:
    - Verizon: Verizon's cellular network coverage extends across much of the United States, with varying levels of coverage in urban, suburban, and rural areas. Coverage quality and availability may vary depending on location.
    - Starlink: Starlink aims to provide global coverage by deploying a network of satellites in low Earth orbit. As of early 2022, Starlink has been expanding its coverage area and is available in select regions worldwide. However, coverage may still be limited in some places, and service availability depends on the user's geographical location and the positioning of satellites overhead.

1. Speed and Performance:

- Verizon: Cellular data speeds offered by Verizon can vary depending on factors such as network congestion, signal strength, and the user's proximity to cell towers. Rates typically range from a few Mbps to over 100 Mbps, depending on the specific cellular technology (e.g., 4G LTE, 5G) and network conditions.
- Starlink: Starlink advertises download speeds ranging from 50 Mbps to 150 Mbps and upload speeds ranging from 10 Mbps to 20 Mbps, with latency ranging from 20ms to 40ms in most locations. Actual rates and performance may vary based on user location, network congestion, and atmospheric conditions.

1. Use Cases:
   - Verizon: Verizon's cellular data services are commonly used for mobile connectivity, including smartphones, tablets, mobile hotspots, and Internet devices. It's suitable for users needing on-the-go internet access or connectivity in areas with limited wired broadband options.
   - Starlink: StarLink's satellite internet service is aimed at users in rural or remote areas where traditional wired or cellular internet options may be unavailable or inadequate. It's also suitable for users who require high-speed internet access for activities such as remote work, online education, or streaming media.

In summary, while Verizon and Starlink offer data network services, they utilize different technologies and cater to other use cases and customer demographics. Verizon primarily offers cellular data services nationwide, while Starlink provides satellite internet service focusing on global coverage and serving underserved or remote areas.

Appendix E

Data Backup Services

Numerous data backup services are available, each offering different features, storage options, and pricing plans. Here are some popular data backup services:

1. Google Drive: Google Drive offers cloud storage and backup services, allowing users to store files, documents, photos, and more. It includes automatic syncing, file versioning, and collaboration tools.
2. Dropbox: Dropbox is a cloud storage and file synchronization service that offers automatic backup and file versioning features. It's famous for its ease of use and compatibility with various devices and operating systems.
3. Microsoft OneDrive: OneDrive is Microsoft's cloud storage service, which integrates seamlessly with Windows and Office applications. It offers automatic backup, file versioning, and collaboration features.
4. Apple iCloud: iCloud is Apple's cloud storage service, primarily aimed at iOS and macOS users. It offers automatic backup for photos, videos, documents, and device settings across Apple devices.
5. Amazon S3: Amazon Simple Storage Service (S3) is a scalable cloud storage service provided by Amazon Web Services (AWS). It's designed for developers and businesses that require highly durable and scalable storage solutions.
6. Backblaze: Backblaze offers unlimited cloud backup for personal and business users. It automatically backs up files and folders on Windows and macOS devices with continuous or scheduled backup options.
7. Carbonite: Carbonite provides cloud backup solutions for individuals and businesses, offering features such as automatic backup, file versioning, and remote access to files.
8. Acronis True Image: Acronis True Image is a comprehensive backup and recovery solution offering full image backups, file synchronization, and ransomware protection.
9. IDrive: IDrive offers cloud backup and storage solutions for individuals

and businesses, with continuous data protection, file versioning, and hybrid backup options.

10. CrashPlan: CrashPlan provides automatic cloud backup for personal and business users, offering unlimited storage and file versioning features.

These are just a few examples of data backup services available. When choosing a backup service, consider storage capacity, pricing, ease of use, security features, and compatibility with your devices and operating systems. Additionally, it's essential to regularly review and test your backup strategy to ensure that your data is protected and recoverable in case of data loss or disaster.

Appendix F

Data Management Tools and Applications

Several types of data management tools and applications are available for RVers looking to manage their data usage effectively. These tools can help RVers monitor their data consumption, track usage patterns, and avoid exceeding data limits. Here are some examples:

1. Mobile Carrier Apps: Many mobile carriers offer dedicated applications that allow users to monitor their data usage in real-time. These apps typically provide information on use, remaining data allowances, and billing details. Examples include the My Verizon, MyAT&T, and T-Mobile apps.

2. Data Monitoring Apps: Various third-party apps for Android and iOS devices can help RVers monitor their data usage. These apps track data usage across all apps and services on the device, providing detailed breakdowns and usage alerts. Examples include My Data Manager, Data Usage Monitor, and 3G Watchdog.

3. Router Management Tools: Some Wi-Fi routers used in RVs come with built-in data management features that allow users to monitor and control data usage. These tools may offer options to set data limits, track usage by device, and prioritize certain types of traffic. Users can typically access these features through a web interface or dedicated mobile app provided by the router manufacturer.

4. Wi-Fi Signal Boosters: Wi-Fi signal boosters can help improve the quality and reliability of Wi-Fi connections in RVs, which can be particularly useful when relying on the campground or public Wi-Fi networks. While not directly related to data management, better Wi-Fi connectivity can help RVers optimize their data usage by ensuring faster and more stable internet connections.

5. Satellite Internet Monitoring Tools: For RVers using satellite internet services, some satellite internet providers offer online portals or apps that allow users to monitor their data usage and account status. These

tools provide information on use, remaining data allowances, and account billing details.

6. Cloud-based Data Tracking Services: Some services offer cloud-based data tracking and monitoring tailored to RVers and travelers. These services typically provide customizable data usage alerts, usage history tracking, and recommendations for optimizing data usage while on the road.

By using these data management tools and applications, RVers can keep track of their data usage more effectively, avoid unexpected overage charges, and make informed decisions about their internet usage while traveling.

Appendix G

Companies that Provide Internet Connections

Satellite Internet Companies

◈ HughesNet offers affordable plans with speeds ranging from 15 to 100 Mbps and unlimited. The program starts at $49.99 mo.

◈ Viasat: Provides faster speeds (12–100 Mbps) but costs more. The data[1][2]. Starts at $99.99 mo.

◈ Starlink is known for unlimited high-speed data (5–220 Mbps) but has a steep initial hardware cost (around $600)[3]. It starts at $120/mo.

---

1. https://www.bing.com/aclk?ld=e8X6pmKs-

jtINmS9HJef0CXjVUCUw9NGnc1HHfTGcfhOFHydduXKiTU0THT9gYURYZ6I7eSzGfGCs1qNLq

Ou3D2FGOr6Zjm9B7OLv9SjQjrPUwAS1ydJF5rIRZ4WkTI66T0Txwvyb4by7n_qOCunpSX067KUJNN

KVRuwSR77Un0G6VgUaW&u=aHR0cHMlM2ElMmYlMmZ3d3cudmVyaXpvbi5jb20lMmZob21lJTJma

W50ZXJuZXQlMmY1ZyUyZiUzZmNtcCUzZEtOQ19IX1BfQ09FX0JJTl81R0hfMjAyNF8wMl9OQi0x

NTIzNyUyNmtwaWQlM2RiaV9jbXAtNjc1ODg3NzkkwX2FkZy0xMjQwMjUwMTQxMjE2MjA2X2FkLTc

3NTE1NzY1OTc2ODg5X2t3ZC03NzUxNTkxNzkyMzYyOF9kZXYtY19leHQtJTdkiZXh0ZW5zaW9uaW

QlN2Rfc2lnLLTBiZmM4MDU1MjkzNTExMjFiZDJlZTViMzNlNGM0YTBiJTI2dXRtX2lkJTNkYmlfY2

1wLTY3NTg4Nzc5MF9hZGctMTI0MDI1MDE0MTIxNjIwNl9hZC03NzUxNTc2NTk3Njg4OV9rd2Qt

Nzc1MTU5MTc5MjM2MjhfZGV2LWNfZXh0LV9wcmQtX3NpZy0wYmZjODA1NTI5MzUxMTIxYm

QyZWU1YjMzZTRjNGEwYiUyNnNpZ25JTI2dXRtX3Rlcm0lM2RiaW5nJTI2dXRtX3Rlcm0lM2RiaV9jbXAtNjc

1ODg3NzkwX2FkZy0xMjQwMjUwMTQxMjE2MjA2X2FkLTc3NTE1NzY1OTc2ODg5X2t3ZC03NzUx

NTkxNzkyMzYyOF9kZXYtY19leHQtX3ByZC1fc2lnLTBiZmM4MDU1MjkzNTExMjFiZDJlZTViMzNl

NGM0YTBiJTI2bXNjbGtpZCUzZDBiZmM4MDU1MjkzNTExMjFiZDJlZTViMzNlNGM0YTBiJTI2

dXRtX211ZGl1bSUzZGNwYyUyUyNnV0bV9jYW1wYWlnbiUzZEJOR19WQ0dfSE9NRS01R19TUkNfRU

4tRU5fU09VVEhfUEhSX05tCX0dFTl9JTlQtMjAyNCUyNnV0bV9jb250ZW50JTNkUEhSX05tCX0dFT

19JTlRfR0VO&rlid=0bfc805529351121bd2ee5b33e4c4a0b

2. https://www.satelliteinternet.com/resources/satellite-internet-pros-and-cons/

3. https://www.bing.com/aclk?ld=e8X6pmKs-

jtINmS9HJef0CXjVUCUw9NGnc1HHfTGcfhOFHydduXKiTU0THT9gYURYZ6I7eSzGfGCs1qNLq

Campground Internet Providers

Several companies offer internet services tailored explicitly for campgrounds. Some campgrounds allow free Internet connections, while others charge. Some services are available at many campgrounds, enabling you to use the same account for those participating. Campgrounds.

Some of these companies include:

- Xelogic
- Pickmyrouter.com[4]
- RV Network Admin[5]
- Camplink
- Technologies LLC
- TengoInternet
- CR Network LLC[6]
- Campground Connect
- GuestNet Solutions
- RV Park Wi-Fi

Ou3D2FGOr6Zjm9B7OLv9SjQjrPUwAS1ydJF5rIRZ4WkTI66T0Txwvyb4by7n_qOCunpSX067KUJNN KVRuwSR77Un0G6VgUaW&u=aHR0cHMlM2ElMmYlMmZ3d3cudmVyaXpvbi5jb20lMmZob21lJTJma W50ZXJuZXQlMmY1ZyUyZiUzZmNtcCUzZEtOQ19IX1BfQ09FX0JJTl81R0hfMjAyNF8wMl9OQi0x NTIzNyUyNmtwaWQlM2RiaV9jbXAtNjc1ODg3NzkwX2FkZy0xMjQwMjUwMTQxMjE2MjA2X2FkLTc 3NTE1NzY1OTc2ODg5X2t3ZC03NzUxNTkxNzkyMzYyOF9kZXYtY19leHQtJTddiZXh0ZW5zaW9uaW QlN2Rfc2lnLLTBiZmM4MDU1MjkzNTExMjFiZDJlZTViMzNlNGM0YTBiJTI2dXRtX2lkJTNkYmlfY2 1wLTY3NTg4Nzc5MF9hZGctMTI0MDI1MDE0MTIxNjIwNl9hZC03NzUxNTc2NTk3Njg4OV9rd2QtQt Nzc1MTU5MTc5MjM2Mjhf ZGV2LWNfZXh0LV9wcmQtX3NpZy0wYmZjODA1NTI5MzUxMTIxYm QyZWU1YjMzZTRjNGEwYiUyNnV0bV9zb3VyY2UlM2RiaW5nJTI2dXRtX3Rlcm0lM2RiaV9jbXAtNjc 1ODg3NzkwX2FkZy0xMjQwMjUwMTQxMjE2MjA2X2FkLTc3NTE1NzY1OTc2ODg5X2t3ZC03NzUx NTkxNzkyMzYyOF9kZXYtY19leHQtX3ByZC1fc2lnLTBiZmM4MDU1MjkzNTExMjFiZDJlZTViMzNl NGM0YTBiJTI2bXNjbGtpZCUzZDBiZmM4MDU1MjkzNTExMjFiZDJlZTViMzNlNGM0YTBiJTI2 dXRtX21lZGl1bSUzZGNwYyUyNnV0bV9jYW1wYWlnbiUzZEJOR19WQ0dfSE9NRS01R19TUkNfRU 4tRU5fU09VVEhfUEhfSX05CX0dFTl9JTlQtMjAyNCUyNnV0bV9jb250ZW50JTNkUEhfSX05CX0dFT l9JTlRfR0VO&rlid=0bfc805529351121bd2ee5b33e4c4a0b

4. https://www.zoominfo.com/c/pickmyroutercom/536931383

5. https://www.zoominfo.com/c/home-network-admin/390190348

6. https://www.zoominfo.com/c/cr-network-llc/467331727

- NomadISP
- Xscapers
- RV Wi-Fi Solutions.
- RV Resort Wi-Fi

These companies typically work closely with campground owners and managers to design and implement internet solutions that meet the unique needs of their facilities and guests. Additionally, they often provide ongoing technical support and maintenance to ensure reliable connectivity for campers and RVers.

Yes, there are instances where campgrounds share internet services or collaborate to provide connectivity to their guests. This approach is prevalent in areas where individual campgrounds may need more access to high-speed internet infrastructure or face challenges in delivering reliable connectivity. By sharing internet services, campgrounds can collectively enhance the quality and availability of internet access for their guests. Here are some ways in which campgrounds may share internet services:

Cellular Providers

Here's a list of major cellular companies in the United States:

1. Verizon Wireless
2. AT&T Mobility
3. T-Mobile US
4. Sprint Corporation (Now merged with T-Mobile US)
5. US Cellular
6. C Spire Wireless
7. TracFone Wireless
8. Boost Mobile (A subsidiary of Dish Network)
9. Cricket Wireless (A subsidiary of AT&T)
10. Metro by T-Mobile (Formerly MetroPCS, now part of T-Mobile US)

Appendix H

Telecommunication Companies With Own Cell Towers

Many telecommunications companies worldwide own and operate cell towers to provide cellular data services to their customers. Here are some notable examples:

1. AT&T: AT&T is one of the largest telecommunications companies in the United States and operates its extensive network of cell towers to provide cellular data services to its customers.

2. Verizon: Verizon is another significant telecommunications company in the United States with its network of cell towers. It offers cellular data services under its Verizon Wireless brand.

3. T-Mobile: T-Mobile is a major player in the telecommunications industry and operates its network of cell towers to provide cellular data services. T-Mobile also owns Metro by T-Mobile, a prepaid wireless service.

4. Sprint (now part of T-Mobile): Sprint was a major telecommunications company in the United States before being acquired by T-Mobile. It had its network of cell towers to provide cellular data services to its customers.

5. Telefónica: Telefónica is a multinational telecommunications company based in Spain. It operates its network of cell towers in several countries, including Spain, Germany, the United Kingdom, and Latin America.

6. Vodafone: Vodafone is a multinational telecommunications company in the United Kingdom. It operates its network of cell towers in multiple countries across Europe, Africa, Asia, and Oceania.

7. China Mobile: China Mobile is the largest telecommunications company in China and operates an extensive network of cell towers to provide cellular data services to its customers.

8. NTT Docomo: NTT Docomo is a major telecommunications company in Japan. It operates a network of cell towers to provide

cellular data services to its customers.

These are just a few examples. Many other telecommunications companies worldwide operate cell tower networks to provide cellular data services to their customers.

Appendix I

Some National Chains that Offer FREE Internet

McDonald's
Starbucks
Panera:
Dunkin' Donuts:
Chick-fil-A,
IHOP
Taco Bell
Wendy's also offers free Wi-Fi.
Burger King
Subway (select locations)
Krispy Kreme
Retailers:
Apple Store
Best Buy:
Barnes and Noble (in the café; some in-store)
Lowes
Macy's
Michaels
Nordstrom
Office Depot
Safeway
Sam's Club
Staples
Target
Whole Foods
Marriott: Many Marriott
hotels provide free Wi-Fi in common areas and guest rooms.
Hilton: Hilton hotels offer
Complimentary
Wi-Fi for guests.

Holiday Inn
Sheraton
Hyatt
Fast Food and Cafes:
Tim Hortons
Peet's Coffee.
Au Bon Pain.
Einstein Bros. Bagels
Caribou Coffee
Publix
Kroger
Walmart
Costco (in the food court
area)
Bookstores and Libraries:
Books-A-Million.
Public libraries: Most public
libraries offer free Wi-Fi to visitors.
Other Chains:
EZ Lube Oil Change
Grease Monkey
Jiffy Lube

Appendix J

Off-Grid Options

When you're off the grid or in remote areas without access to traditional wired or cellular internet services, several alternative options exist for staying connected. The best internet options in such situations often depend on location, available resources, and specific connectivity needs. Here are some of the most common options:

1. Satellite Internet: Satellite internet is one of the most widely available options for off-grid connectivity. It relies on satellites orbiting the Earth to provide internet access, making it accessible virtually anywhere with a clear sky view. While satellite internet can be slower and more expensive than other options, it offers reliable connectivity in remote locations where other options may not be available.

2. Cellular Data: If you have a cellular signal in your off-grid location, you can use cellular data to access the internet. This typically requires a mobile hotspot device or a smartphone with tethering capabilities. While cellular data coverage can vary depending on your location and service provider, it's often faster and more affordable than satellite internet.

3. Fixed Wireless: Fixed wireless internet uses radio signals to deliver high-speed internet access to RVs and businesses in rural and remote areas. It involves installing a small antenna on your property to receive alerts from a nearby tower. While availability may be limited in some places, fixed wireless can provide reliable and relatively fast internet service when other options are unavailable.

4. Mesh Networks: Mesh networks are decentralized networks consisting of interconnected nodes that communicate with each other to provide internet access. In off-grid settings, mesh networks can be set up using specialized hardware and software to create a local network for sharing internet access among multiple users. This option suits small communities, campsites, or remote work locations.

5. Long-Range Wi-Fi: Long-range Wi-Fi antennas can establish point-to-point or point-to-multi-point connections over long distances. This option requires line-of-sight between the transmitter and receiver and can provide internet access from remote locations to nearby access points or hotspots.

6. Low-Earth Orbit (LEO) Satellite Constellations: Emerging technologies such as LEO satellite constellations, like SpaceX's Starlink, promise to revolutionize off-grid connectivity by providing high-speed internet access via networks of low-orbiting satellites. While still in the early stages of deployment, these systems have the potential to offer fast, low-latency internet access to even the most remote locations.

When choosing the best internet option for off-grid use, consider coverage, speed, reliability, cost, and equipment requirements. It's also important to research local regulations, terrain, and environmental conditions that may affect connectivity.

Appendix K

Smart Infrastructure

Smart infrastructure refers to integrating advanced technologies, data analytics, and intelligent systems into traditional infrastructure systems to enhance efficiency, sustainability, safety, and overall functionality. It involves leveraging digital connectivity, sensors, and automation to optimize the performance and management of various infrastructure components, such as transportation networks, utilities, buildings, and public spaces.

Critical characteristics of smart infrastructure include:

1. Data Collection and Analysis: Smart infrastructure utilizes sensors and (Internet devices to collect real-time data on infrastructure performance, including traffic flow, energy consumption, environmental conditions, and structural health. This data is then analyzed to gain insights and inform decision-making processes.

2. Integration and Connectivity: Smart infrastructure systems are interconnected through digital platforms and communication networks, enabling seamless coordination and information exchange between different components. This integration facilitates better coordination and efficiency across infrastructure systems.

3. Automation and Control: Automation technologies, such as artificial intelligence (AI) and machine learning, automate routine tasks and optimize system operations. This includes automated control of traffic signals, energy management systems, and predictive maintenance of infrastructure assets.

4. Sustainability and Resilience: Smart infrastructure aims to minimize resource consumption, reduce environmental impact, and enhance resilience to natural disasters and other disruptions. This may involve incorporating renewable energy sources, implementing energy-efficient technologies, and designing infrastructure with climate change adaptation in mind.

5. Enhanced User Experience: By leveraging digital technologies and data-

driven insights, smart infrastructure can improve the overall user experience for citizens, businesses, and government agencies. This includes providing real-time information to travelers, optimizing public service delivery, and enhancing public safety.

Examples of intelligent infrastructure initiatives include:

- Smart transportation systems include intelligent traffic management systems, connected and autonomous vehicles (CAVs), and innovative public transit systems.
- Smart energy grids optimize energy generation, distribution, and consumption through advanced metering, demand response, and distributed energy resources.
- Smart buildings equipped with sensors and automation systems to optimize energy usage, improve occupant comfort, and reduce operating costs.
- Smart water management systems that monitor and control water distribution networks detect leaks, and optimize water usage.
- Smart city initiatives that integrate various infrastructure systems and services to improve overall urban livability, sustainability, and resilience.

Smart infrastructure plays a crucial role in addressing modern cities and communities' evolving challenges, driving innovation, efficiency, and sustainability in managing critical infrastructure assets.

Appendix L

Here's how a router works

Routing Is a Popular Term: Routers use routing tables to determine the best path for forwarding data packets between networks. Each router maintains a routing table containing information about neighboring routers and the network addresses they can reach. When a data packet arrives at a router, it examines the destination IP address and consults its routing table to determine where to forward the packet.

Network Address Translation (NAT): Many routers also perform network address translation, allowing multiple LAN devices to share a single public IP address. When data packets travel between the LAN and the internet, the router translates the private IP addresses of the devices on the LAN into a single public IP address and vice versa. This helps conserve public IP addresses and adds a layer of security by hiding the internal network structure from the outside world.

Firewalls Protect You: Routers often include firewall capabilities to protect the local network from unauthorized access and malicious activity. The firewall can be configured to filter incoming and outgoing traffic based on predefined rules, such as allowing or blocking specific types of traffic or restricting access to certain IP addresses or ports.

Wireless Access Point (WAP): Many modern routers also include a built-in wireless access point, which allows devices to connect to the router using Wi-Fi instead of wired Ethernet connections. The router acts as a bridge between the wired and wireless networks, allowing devices connected to the LAN to communicate with wireless devices and vice versa.

DHCP server assigns IPs: Routers often include a DHCP (Dynamic Host Configuration Protocol) server, which automatically gives IP addresses to devices on the local network. When a device connects to the web, it sends a DHCP request to the router, which responds with an available IP address, subnet mask, gateway address, and other network configuration parameters.

Overall, a router plays a crucial role in managing network traffic, facilitating communication between devices on the LAN, and providing access to the internet. It acts as a gateway between the local network and the wider internet, ensuring data packets are routed efficiently and securely.

Appendix M

Cellular Data Connections

Here's how a cellular data connection works:

1. Radio Communication: Mobile devices, such as smartphones, tablets, or hotspot devices, contain a cellular modem communicating with nearby cell towers using radio waves.
2. Cellular Networks: Cell towers are strategically placed to provide coverage within their respective "cells." Each building communicates with nearby devices and routes their data to and from the wider internet.
3. Data Transmission: When a device sends or receives data, such as browsing the web, streaming video, or using apps, the data is transmitted wirelessly between the device and the nearest cell tower.
4. Mobile Network Infrastructure: The data is then routed through the telecommunications company's network infrastructure, which may involve multiple connection points, switches, and servers.
5. Internet Access: Eventually, the data reaches its destination online (e.g., a website server or online service), and the requested information is sent back to the device via the same process in reverse.
6. Cellular data connections offer mobility and convenience, allowing users to access the internet from almost anywhere within the coverage area of their mobile network provider. They are commonly used for web browsing, email, social media, streaming audio/video, online gaming, and more.

Cellular data connections are typically billed by the amount of data transferred (data usage) or as part of a monthly data plan. Users should be mindful of their data usage to avoid exceeding their plan's data limits and incurring additional charges. Additionally, the speed and reliability of cellular data connections can vary depending on factors such as network congestion, signal strength, and geographic location.

Appendix N

Cellular Coverage Maps

Since Satellites provide coverage all over the US, it is unnecessary to show their range. Since the four major cellular companies use cell towers to send signals, none provide complete data and voice coverage. When deciding what coverage would work best for you, verify that there is strong coverage where you travel.

Below are links to two different maps that show the coverage available:

CoverageMap.com:

- This website provides verified and estimated coverage maps for all carriers.
- CoverageMap.com[1].

UpPhone Coverage Map:

- You can type your address into the search box to discover which carriers provide coverage in your county, town, neighborhood, or backyard.
- Compare wireless carriers' coverage using their voice, 3G, and LTE coverage maps.

---

1. https://www.coveragemap.com/

Appendix O

Some Wi-Fi Boosters and Extenders

Below is a list of ever-changing Wi-Fi Boosters and Extenders, so I suggest you do a Google search to discover any new ones that have come on the market. Be sure to look at their ratings. Also, talk to other RVers about their use and the pros and Cons.

- Google Wi-Fi System AC 1200:
    - This mesh Wi-Fi system provides coverage throughout your RV. It's easy to set up and offers reliable performance.
- KING KF1000 Falcon Automatic Wi-Fi Range Extender:
    - Designed for RVs, this rooftop antenna extends your Wi-Fi range significantly. It's automatic and hassle-free.
- NETGEAR RV Wi-Fi Range Extender EX6120:
    - This compact extender is cost-effective and improves Wi-Fi coverage in your RV.
- Alfa Wi-Fi Camp Pro 2 Long Range Wi-Fi Repeater RV Kit:
    - Ideal for remote locations, this kit includes an outdoor antenna and a powerful repeater.

- Winegard WF-4035 Black ODU Extender:
    - Easy to install, this extender enhances Wi-Fi coverage without complications.
- Bear Extender RV & Marine USB Outdoor Wi-Fi Antenna:
    - Designed for outdoor use, this USB antenna withstands various weather conditions.
- Alfa AWUS036NH USB Wireless Wi-Fi Network Adapter:
    - Compact and versatile, this USB adapter improves Wi-Fi reception.
- D-Link AC1750 Wi-Fi Range Extender:
    - This extender plugs directly into an outlet, making it convenient for RVs.

Your best choice depends on your needs, budget, and travel habits. Whether you work remotely, stream movies, or stay connected, these Wi-Fi boosters can significantly enhance your RV internet experience! Just be sure to look at the reviews and see what issues customers are having.

Appendix P

Magazines, TV Shows, Clubs & Sites About RVing

I love this industry and would like to share where you can learn more about it!
Paid RV Magazine Subscriptions

- I Heart RVing Magazine[1]
- RV Today Magazine[2]
- Family RVing Magazine[3]
- RV Destinations Magazine[4]
- RV Enthusiast Magazine[5]
- RV Lifestyle Magazine[6]
- Snowbirds & Travelers RV Magazine[7]
- Wildsam RV Magazine[8]
- Vintage Trailer Magazine (not a secured site)

Free RV Magazine Subscriptions

- RV America Magazine[9]
- RV Camping Magazine[10]
- Go RV Magazine[11]

---

1. https://iheartrving.com/

2. https://rvtoday.com/

3. https://familyrvingmag.com/

4. https://rvdestinationsmagazine.com/

5. https://rventhusiast.com/

6. https://www.rvlifemag.com/

7. https://suncruisermedia.com/Home

8. https://www.wildsam.com/magazine

9. https://rvamericamagazine.com/

10. https://issuu.com/rvcampingmagazine/docs/rvcm_0622

11. https://www.gorving.com/?utm_source=google&utm_medium=cpc&utm_campaign=brand&utm_term=g

   oing-

- RVBusiness[12]

RV Business Magazine

- RV News Business Magazine[13]
- Woodhall's RV Campground Magazine[14]
- RV Dealer News Magazine[15]
- RV Pro Magazine[16]

Industry Organizations and Manufacturers

- RV Industry Association (RVIA):[17]
- North American RV Manufacturers[18]:

RV Clubs and Associations:

These organizations provide resources, community, and support for RV enthusiasts:

- Escapees RV Club[19]: Established in the 1970s, it's one of the oldest RV membership organizations.
- Family Motor Coach Association (FMCA):[20] Offers community discounts and resources for travelers.
- Good Sam Club[21]: Provides benefits, discounts, and services to RVers.

---

rving&utm_content=phrase&gclsrc=aw.ds&ds_rl=1285337&ds_rl=1286131&gad_source=1&ds_rl=1285 337&ds_rl=1286131&gclid=Cj0KCQiArrCvBhCNARIsAOkAGcXIGq4nWJiEGUV2exlPdwAP_UZLD PJru7Wrdm5x5FSeHvmn4ct7PuwaAtUzEALw_wcB&gclsrc=aw.ds

12. https://rvbusiness.com/

13. https://www.rvnews.com/

14. https://woodallscm.com/

15. https://rvldealernews.com/

16. https://rv-pro.com/magazine/

17. https://www.rvia.org/

18. https://campaddict.com/rv-manufacturers/

19. https://escapees.com/

20. https://www.fmca.com/

- Harvest Hosts[22]: Connects RVers with unique overnight stays at wineries, farms, and more.
- Passport America[23]: Offers discounted camping rates at participating campgrounds.
- Mobile Internet Resources[24]: Focuses on staying connected while on the road.

RV Forums and Group Pages

New groups and forums are constantly being created. A simple Google or Facebook search will update you on the latest ones.

- Facebook: Living the RV Dream[25]
- Facebook: Internet For RVers[26]
- Facebook: Workamping for Full Time RVers[27]
- Facebook: Full-Time RVers[28]

◈ Facebook: RV Newbies[29]:
◈ Facebook: North American RV Travel[30]:

21. https://www.goodsam.com/club/
join?utm_source=google&utm_medium=ppc&utm_campaign=%5Badv:+Membership%5D+%5Bplt:+Goo
gle%5D+%5Bfun:+Performance%5D+%5Bini:+Good+Sam%5D+%5Btgt:+Brand%5D+%5Bbil:+Direct%
5D&GSOFFER=ppc&cq_cmp=2074824881&cq_con=76271081933&cq_term=good%20sam%20club&c
q_plac=&cq_net=g&cq_plt=gp&gad_source=1&gclid=Cj0KCQiArrCvBhCNARIsAOkAGcWWzaRkBD
NDwzmhxmpa27xPV5WDGJfJpkBkgW-R0E0WnsghByKnf8oaAnCEEALw_wcB&gclsrc=aw.ds

22. https://harvesthosts.com/join-
now/?gad_source=1&gclid=Cj0KCQiArrCvBhCNARIsAOkAGcVJm6P9gl_e5sVvFAtbopAYIttOeDIq8-
53-JpUaDnJvP5Q84CC3bgaAjLhEALw_wcB

23. https://passportamerica.com/

24. https://www.rvmobileinternet.com/

25. https://www.facebook.com/search/top?q=living%20the%20rv%20dream

26. https://www.facebook.com/groups/374108812691682

27. https://www.facebook.com/groups/workamping

28. https://www.facebook.com/groups/fulltimeRVing

29. https://www.facebook.com/groups/rvingnewbies

◇ Facebook: Fulltime Families[31]:
◇ Facebook: FREE RV Campgrounds[32]

- Facebook: RV Lifestyle Group[33]
- Facebook: RVing Women[34]: A social site for RVers
- RV Forum[35]
- iRV2 Forums[36]
- RV Network[37] (Escapees)

---

30. https://www.facebook.com/groups/426609654336620

31. https://www.facebook.com/groups/FulltimeFamilies

32. https://www.facebook.com/groups/freecampgrounds

33. https://www.facebook.com/groups/roadtreking

34. https://www.facebook.com/RVingWomen

35. https://www.rvforum.net/

36. https://www.irv2.com/forums/

37. https://www.rvnetwork.com/

Don't miss out!

Visit the website below and you can sign up to receive emails whenever Wes "Wheels" Wheeler publishes a new book. There's no charge and no obligation.

https://books2read.com/r/B-A-YOWGB-NXCBD

About the Author

Wes "Wheels" Wheeler is a seasoned adventurer, passionate RV enthusiast, and prolific author dedicated to exploring the wonders of RVing and sharing valuable insights with fellow travelers. With years of experience of enjoying the RV lifestyle, Wheels brings a wealth of knowledge and expertise to his writings on RV technology, connectivity, and travel. He loves to research all types of RV topics and has written several books that he is now starting to publish. As a digital nomad, he understands the importance of staying connected while on the move. He is committed to empowering RVers with the tools and information to enhance their journeys. Through his engaging and informative writing style, Wheels inspires readers to embark on their own RV adventures and make the most of their time on the road. Whether uncovering the latest trends in RV internet technology or sharing captivating travel stories, Wheels' passion for exploration and discovery shines through in every word he writes.

Read more at https://www.fancyfreeliving.com.